A Little Book of Limericks

Funny Rhymes for all the Family

Compiled by Hugh Morrison

MONTPELIER PUBLISHING
London
MMXV

ISBN-13: 978-1511524124
ISBN-10: 151152412X
Published by Montpelier Publishing, London.
Printed by Amazon Createspace.

She had blonde hair all tied in a plait
And her friends were all jealous of that,
Until one windy day
Her hat sailed away.
And her hair sailed away with the hat.

There was an old man of Sheerness
Who invited a friend to play chess
But he'd lent all the pieces
To one of his nieces
And stupidly lost her address.

A flea and a fly in a flue
Were imprisoned, so what could they do?
Said the fly, 'Let us flee!'
Said the flea, 'Let us fly!'
So they flew through a flaw in the flue.

A certain young fellow named Beebee
Wished to marry a lady named Phoebe
'But,' said he, 'I must see
What the church service fee
Be before Phoebe be Phoebe Beebee.'

An eccentric old gent, name of Moxon
Rented a farm near Thame, Oxon,
He allowed all his cows
To roam through the house
And the parlour was filled with tame oxen.

There was a young lady named Perkins,
Who had a great fondness for gherkins;
At afternoon tea
She ate twenty-three.
Which pickled her internal workins.

The folk of the Indian nation
Are incredibly keen on cremation
For few can find fault
With a miniscule vault
That contains every single relation.

Since marriage, a woman from Bacup
Has refused to spend money on makeup.
Instead of a lipstick
She uses a dipstick
We're expecting a marital breakup.

There was an old man in a hearse
Who murmured, 'This might have been worse;
Of course the expense
Is simply immense,
But it doesn't come out of my purse.'

A baby in Kalamazoo
Remarked quite distinctly, 'Goo-goo.'
'Twas explained by his ma.
And likewise his pa.
That he meant to say, 'How do you do?'

There was a young fellow named Paul,
Who went to a fancy dress ball;
They say, just for fun
He dressed up like a bun,
And was ate by a dog in the hall

There was an old fellow named Green,
Who grew so abnormally lean,
And flat, and compressed,
That his back touched his chest.
And sideways he couldn't be seen.

I'd rather have fingers than toes,
I'd rather have ears than a nose,
And as for my hair,
I'm glad it's all there,
I'll be awfully sad when it goes.

There was an old man who said, 'How,
Shall I flee from this horrible cow?
I will sit on this stile
And continue to smile.'
I guess he's still sitting there now.

A certain old lady called Rose
In despair, taught her bird to propose;
But the parrot, dejected.
At being accepted,
Shrieked words too profane to disclose.

There was an old man who said, 'Do
Tell me how I'm to add two and two?
I'm not very sure
That it doesn't make four —
But I fear that is almost too few.'

There was an old lady from Fife
Who had never been kissed in her life;
Along came a cat;
And she said, 'I'll kiss that!'
But the cat answered, 'Not on your life!"

There was a young lady of Crete
Who was so exceedingly neat.
When she got out of bed
She stood on her head,
To make sure of not dirtying her feet.

I wish that my room had a floor;
I don't so much care for a door;
But this crawling around
Without touching the ground
Is getting to be quite a bore.

There was a young man from Ostend,
Who vowed he'd hold out to the end;
But when half way over
From Calais to Dover,
He did what he didn't intend

There was a young girl named O'Neill
Who went up in the great Ferris Wheel;
But when half way around
She looked at the ground
And it cost her her previous meal.

There was an old fellow called Aitchison
Whose trousers had many rough patchison;
'I consider them great,'
He'd frequently state,
'For using to strike all my matcheson.'

A silly young fellow named Hyde,
In a funeral procession was spied;
When asked 'Who is dead?'
He giggled and said,
'I don't know; I just came for the ride.'

There once was an old man of Lyme
Who married three wives at a time:
When asked, 'Why a third?'
He replied, 'One's absurd,
And bigamy, sir, is a crime.'

There was an old lady of Brooking,
Who had a great genius for cooking;
She could bake sixty pies
All of quite the same size,
And tell which was which without looking.

There once was a girl of New York,
Whose body was lighter than cork;
She had to be fed
For six weeks upon lead,
Before she went out for a walk.

There was a young lady whose dream
Was to feed a black cat on whipped cream;
But the first cat she found
Spilled the cream on the ground,
And she fed a whipped cat on black cream.

There was an old man of Tobago
Who lived on rice, gruel, and sago;
Till much to his bliss
His physician said this —
To a leg, sir, of mutton you may go.

There was an old fellow called Ghandi
Who went to the pub for a shandy
With his great loin cloth
He wiped off the froth
And the barman said 'Blimey, that's handy!'

There was a young man from Berlin,
Who was so excessively thin,
That when he was made
To drink lemonade
He slipped through the straw and fell in.

There was an old man from Antigua,
Whose wife said, 'My dear, what a pig you are.'
He replied, 'O my queen.
Is it manners you mean?
Or do you refer to my fig-u-a?'

There was a young maid who said, 'Why
Can't I look in my ear with my eye?
If I put my mind to it
I'm sure I can do it:
You never can tell till you try!'

A lady from Chippenham, Wilts,
Once walked up to Scotland on stilts
When they said, 'Oh, how shocking
To show so much stocking!'
She answered, 'Well, how about kilts?'

Said a bad little youngster named Beecham
Those jelly tarts, how shall I reach 'em?
To my parents I'd go.
But they always say no.
No matter how much I beseech 'em!'

The Sultan, annoyed with his harem
Invented a scheme for to scare 'em;
He caught him a mouse
Which he loosed in the house;
The confusion was called 'harem-scarem'.

A tutor who tooted the flute,
Tried to teach two young fluters to toot;
Said the two to the tutor,
'Is it harder to toot, or
To tutor two fluters to toot?'

A canner, exceedingly canny.
One morning remarked to his granny,
'A canner can can
Anything that he can.
But a canner can't can a can, can he?'

There was a young lady of Niger
Who smiled as she rode on a tiger
They returned from the ride
With the lady inside,
And the smile on the face of the tiger.

There was a young man of St. Kitts
Who was very much troubled with fits;
The eclipse of the moon
Threw him into a swoon;
When he tumbled and broke into bits

There was a young person named Ned,
Who dined before going to bed.
On lobster and ham
And salad and jam,
And when he awoke he was dead.

There once was a pious young priest,
Who lived almost wholly on yeast;
'For,' he said, 'it is plain,
We must all rise again,
And I want to get started, at least.'

To his wife said a person named Brown
My dear, there's a caller from town.'
'Wait!' she cried in distress,
'Til I slip on a dress,'
But she slipped on the stairs and came down.

There was a young lady whose eyes,
Were unique as to colour and size;
When she opened them wide,
People all turned aside,
And started away in surprise.

There was a young woman named Florence,
Who for kissing professed great abhorrence;
But when she'd been kissed
And found what she'd missed.
She cried till the tears came in torrents.

There was a young person called Kate
Who sat on the stairs very late.
When asked how she fared,
She said she was scared.
But was otherwise doing first-rate.

There once was a man from Nantucket
Who kept all his cash in a bucket.
But his daughter named Nan
Ran away with a man,
And alas for the bucket, Nan-tuck-et.

There was a young girl from New York,
Whose Pa made a fortune in pork;
He bought for his daughter
A tutor who taught her
To balance green peas on her fork.

There was a young man so benighted,
He never knew when he was slighted;
He would go to a party,
And eat just as hearty,
As if he'd been really invited.

There were three young women of Birmingham
And I know a sad story concerning 'em;
They stuck needles and pins
In the Right Reverend shins
Of the Bishop engaged in confirming 'em.

There was an old monk of Siberia,
Whose existence grew drearier and drearier;
He burst from his cell
With a hell of a yell,
And eloped with the Mother Superior.

There was a young poet in Wemyss,
Who cried, 'O, how awful it seems,
When asleep late at night.
Lovely poetry to write,
And awakening find it's but dreymss!'

A man who was steering a yacht,
His course through the water forgacht,
And he stuck in the mud
With a dull, sickening thud.
And the captain then swore a whole lacht.

A composer who lived in the ghetto.
Once wrote out a comic libretto;
When nobody sang it.
He said, 'Oh, well, hang it,
I'll sing it myself in falsetto!'

A war correspondent named Guido
Was struck by a flying torpedo;
A Red Cross brigade
Which came to his aid
Found only a sleeveless tuxedo.

There lived in the village of Beaulieu
A couple who'd gone there but neaulieu;
Their child was named Vaughan
As soon as 'twas baughan,
But, alas, he proved treaulieu unreaulieu.

There once was an old man in Wemyss,
Used to dream such remarkable dremyss,
The folks stared aghast
At the things he'd forecast
And give vent to their terror in scremyss.

There was a young man from Elora,
Who married a girl called Lenora,
But he had not been wed
Very long till he said,
'Oh, drat it! I've married a snorer!'

An oyster from Kalamazoo
Confessed he was feeling quite blue,
'For,' says he, 'as a rule.
When the weather turns cool,
I invariably get in a stew!'

A king who began on his reign.
Exclaimed with a feeling of peign,
'Though I'm legally heir,
No one seems to ceir
That I haven't been born with a breign.'

There was a young man of Devizes,
Whose ears were two different sizes,
The one that was small
Was no use at all,
But the other won several prizes.

There once was a corpulent carp,
Who wanted to play on a harp,
But to his chagrin,
So short was his fin
That he couldn't reach up to C sharp.

Said a bicycling fellow, 'Now, then,
I will ride like the real racing men!'
But he got into trouble,
For he bent himself double.
And couldn't bend back again.

There was a young fellow who sat
Quite thoughtlessly flat on his hat.
He reposed there a while
And so altered its style,
That he uses it now for a mat.

I know a disgusting old man,
Who eats just as much as he can.
He covers his vest
With remains of the best
Of the gravy and chicken and ham.

There once was a wonderful ape.
Who gave up his fur for a cape.
Now he swings in the trees,
All exposed to the breeze,
Which leaves him in very bad shape.

'There's a train at 4.04,' said Miss Jenny,
'Four tickets I'll take. Have you any?'
Said the man at the door,
'Not four for 4.04,
For four for 4.04 are too many.'

Six Sikhs asked the steward to fix
Them a nice little stew at 6.06,
But the wind blew a gale.
And they rushed to the rail,
For six Sikhs were seasick at 6.06.

The inventor, he chortled with glee,
As they fished his spaceship from the sea,
'I shall build,' and he laughed,
'A submarine craft,
And, perhaps, it will fly,' remarked he.

There was an old lady of Rye,
Who was baked by mistake in a pie,
To the household's disgust
She emerged through the crust.
And exclaimed, with a yawn, 'Where am I?'

An inventor flew up from Rangoon
On a flying machine to the moon;
He has not yet come back,
And his wife, who's in black,
Hopes to draw his insurance cheque soon.

A certain young fellow named Robbie
Rode his horse back and forth in the lobby;
When they told him, 'Indoors
Is no place for a horse,'
He replied, 'Well, you see, it's my hobby.'

There was a young person named Billy
Whose actions were what you'd call silly;
At a fancy dress ball
He wore nothing at all
Pretending to represent Chile.

A foolish young chef from Dunoon
Thought he'd sell some green cheese to the moon
So he flew up one night
But got a great fright
When the moon said 'Don't be a buffoon!'

A certain young woman named Hannah
Slipped down on a piece of banana,
She shrieked and 'oh, my'd'.
And more stars she spied
Than belong to the star-spangled banner.

In a rainstorm a girl of renown
Insisted on going downtown.
But the umbrella's leaks
Wet the bloom on her cheeks,
And it dropped down and ruined her gown.

As we've seen the young girl was no saint.
And she lodged a most mighty complaint;
She raved and she swore
At the man in the store
For not selling her waterproof paint.

There was a young girl of Madrid,
Whose bike went amiss with a skid.
The bike it was broken.
And words they were spoken,
I'm sorry she did, but she did!

There once were two cats from Kilkenny,
Each thought there was one cat too many,
So they fought and they and hit,
They scratched and they bit.
Now instead of two cats, there aren't any.

There once was a lady from Guam
Who said 'Now the sea is so calm
I will swim for a lark,'
But she met with a shark,
Let us now sing the 23rd psalm.

There was a young maid of Manilla,
Whose favorite cream was vanilla.
But sad to relate,
Though you piled up her plate,
'Twas impossible ever to fill her.

A man owned a cow in Nantucket,
She knew a square meal when she struck it.
One night she broke in
To the oats — cleaned the bin,
And the next day this cow kicked the bucket.

There was an old man with a skewer
Who hunted a hostile reviewer,
'I'll teach him,' he cried,
'When I've punctured his hide.
To call my last novel impure.'

There was a fair Philippine maid
Who walked in the streets unarrayed.
When asked why she did it
She replied: 'I should fidget
If dressed, for my best frock is frayed.'

From Paris Maude ordered her bonnet,
'Twas a 'poem,' 'creation,' a 'sonnet,'
But the sight of the bill
Made her dear father ill,
And as for the rampage — he's on it.

A messenger boy named Mercurius,
One day earned a dime that was spurious.
He turned that one in.
Spent the other for gin.
And made his pa, Jupiter, furious.

A certain young man of great gumption,
'Mongst cannibals had the presumption
To go — but, alack!
He never came back.
They say 'twas a case of consumption.

Young Mrs. Hubbard went to the cupboard
To get her some *fromage de brie*.
But none found she there,
Her husband — the bear!
Had gobbled it all up, you see.

'Tis strange how new newspapers honour
The creature that's called *prima donna*;
They say not a thing
Of how she can sing,
But talk of the clothes she has on her.

There was a young lady named Maud,
Who at meals was a terrible fraud.
She never was able
To eat at the table.
But — out in the pantry — oh, Lord!

There once was a bull dog named Caesar,
Saw a cat and thought he would taesar,
But the cat was too fly,
And she scratched out an eye,
Now Caesar just sees her and flaesar.

In the wild West there lived a young Sioux,
Who made quite a brilliant debioux
In highest society,
With all due propriety.
Just as every sweet maiden should dioux.

Never once was her young mind opaque
Whether she was asleep or awaque,
For, at quick repartee,
Either night or by dee,
She was ready to give and to take.

In London a certain girl's bonnet
Has three dozen ostrich plumes on it,
While her sister, poor thing.
Wears an old chicken's wing,
And that is the cause of this sonnet.

There was a young fellow named Snape
Who always wore trousers of crepe,
When asked if they'd tear,
He replied, 'Here and there,
But they hold such an elegant shape.'

There was a sculptor named Phidias,
Whose statues were perfectly hideous,
He made Aphrodite
Without any nightie,
And shocked the ultra-fastidious.

Now when Aphrodite by Phidias
Had shocked the ultra-fastidious,
Then all the old aunties
Swore she must wear panties,
Which made her look perfectly hideous.

And if all the old aunties will squeal-o
Because statues don't wear a great deal-o,
Then for heaven's sake ask
That a loose-fitting basque
Be made for the Venus de Milo!

A young fellow wore some pyjamas.
Made entirely of wool from the llamas.
The unmanly effect
Made people suspect,
That the outfit was really his mama's.

There was a young maiden of Michigan,
To meet her, I never would wish again.
She gobbled ice-cream.
Till with pain she would scream,
Then she would eat a whole dish again.

There was a young lady named Mabel,
Who danced on the dining-room table,
But she blushed very red,
When the gentlemen said,
'Oh! look at the legs on the table.'

A Spaniard whose name was Jose,
Jad justled to get in jis je;
He took off jis jat
And jappily sat
Upon the fence, crying 'Jooray!'

A lady who lived at Bordeaux,
Had a corn on her right little teaux;
She borrowed a razor.
For her skill we must praise her.
For the corn is gone, (so is her teaux).

A farmer once called his cow 'Zephyr,'
She seemed such an amiable heifer.
When the farmer drew near
She kicked off his ear.
And now he's very much dephyr.

Each evening a good looking Mr.
Comes around for to visit my sr.
One night on the stairs,
He, all unawares,
Put his arm round her shoulders and kr.

A boy was so fond of Welsh rabbit
That his taste led him into the habit
Of spending his days
Near the doors of cafes,
And when he would see one he'd grab it.

21

Once a Frenchman who'd promptly said *'Oui'*
To some ladies who'd ask him if houi
Cared to drink, threw a fit
Upon finding that it
Was a tipple no stronger than toui.

There once was a mouse that loved cheese,
But in vain, as the scent made him sneeze,
Till he took some cologne
Well mixed with ozone —
And now he says 'more if you please.'

There was a young girl in the choir
Whose voice rose hoir and hoir,
Till it reached such a height
It was clear out of sight,
And they found it next day in the spoir.

A fool girl of Paris named Jane
Once threw herself into the Seine.
She was off of her head,
The fisherman said
Who found her. He found her in Seine.

The animals down at the Zoo
They didn't know just what to do,
Said the tiger: 'Methinks
That a golf game, by jinks,
Is the thing,' - so they played on the lynx.

A very sad play called 'East Lynne,'
A mixture of virtue and synne;
Big crowds, black and white,
Packed the house every night —
In fact, they could hardly get ynne.

A vessel has sailed from Chicago
With barrels of pork for a cargo;
For Boston she's bound,
Preceded, I've found,
By another with beans from near Fargo.

Of a sudden the great *prima donna*
Cried 'Heavens, my voice is a goner!'
But a cat in the wings
Cried, 'I know how she sings,'
And finished the solo with honour.

There once was a maiden in Florida
Who had no hat, so she borrowed a
Little old bonnet,
Men doted up on it,
But the girls said she couldn't look horrider.

An artist who painted a ceiling,
Remarked, with an air of much feeling,
'The lady is Eve,
And I'd have you believe,
'Tis an apple she seems to be peeling.'

There was a young man named Pete,
Who thought he was very discreet.
Till he met a sweet girl,
Now his brain's in a whirl,
And he can't tell his head from his feet.

There was a young boy of renown
Who left litter all over the town
Til his pa, in a rage
At all this garbage
Dumped the boy in a bin upside down.

A miss was once kissed on her wrist,
Where no miss would like to be kissed;
Said the kissed to the kisser,
'How dare you do this, sir
Now take back that kiss, I insist.'

I should think you could see that you're here.
And you'll always remain here, I fear,
For it matters not where
You may go, when you're there.
You'll say to yourself, 'I am here.'

In New Orleans there lived a young Creole,
Who, when asked if her hair were all reole,
Replied, with a shrug,
'Just give it a tug,
And judge by the way that I squeole.'

A freckled young damsel named Clara
Much wished to grow fairer and fairer;
So she tried cream of tartar,
With the faith of a marytr,
And her freckles grew rarer and rarer.

There was a cross chappie called Charlie,
Whose temper was knotted and gnarly;
He'd say, 'Wake me at eight;'
But would sleep on till late,
Then wake up all snappy and snarly.

He courted a gem of a girl,
And told her that she was his pearl;
But when they were married,
Her ma came and tarried,
And he didn't like mother of pearl.

We once had a blasphemous parrot.
That swore till we just couldn't bear it.
When we tied up his beak.
He learned in one week
In the deaf and dumb language to swear it.

There was an old maiden named White,
Who slept in pajamas one night,
As she happened to pass
Near a large looking-glass.
She exclaimed, 'There's a man!' in delight.

There once was a lady called Proctor
Who owned a bad parrot that mocked her,
He would likewise blaspheme,
Using language extreme —
All of which, the lady said, shocked her.

A man hired by John Smith & Company,
Loudly declared that he'd thump any.
Men that he saw.
Dumping dirt near the store.
The drivers, therefore, didn't dump any.

There was a young lady called Lawrence,
Whose language came gushing in torrents,
Till told by her teacher,
'Your manner, dear creature,
Is more than your scholarship warrants.'

She was at a ball wearing a mask,
And he for her heart tried to ask.
But, behold, 'twas his mother.
Instead of another,
So he never completed his task.

A wondrous faith-healer one day,
Had to turn all his patients away,
To tell you the truth,
He was pained by a tooth,
Which his faith couldn't heal, strange to say.

'Will you dream of me, dear one, tonight?'
She answered — he heard with a thrill:
'You know I've a habit.
Of eating Welsh rabbit,
And it's likely as not that I will.'

There was a young fellow from Lancing,
Who was very devoted to dancing;
He waltzed a girl once.
She called him a dunce,
Because on her toes he kept prancing.

A bookworm of Kennebunk, Maine,
Found pleasure in reading Montaigne,
He also liked Poe,
And Daniel Defoe,
But the telephone book caused him pain.

There was a young man called McLeod,
Who played the trombone far too loud,
He was hit by a boot.
At the very first toot,
But he thanked his detractors and bowed.

A man who was deeply in debt,
Said, 'No matter whatever I gebt.
My creditors claim
A share of the same.
Which makes me discouraged, you bebt.'

He brought home a fancy lawn-mower,
And ran it each morning at four,
But the novelty
Has worn off, and he
Perspires and pushes no mower.

A fellow who lived on the Rhine
Saw a fish and decided to dine.
But how to invite him? —
'Ah,' he said, 'I will write him!'
So he sat down and dropped him a line!

There was an old man up in Maine,
Who stood all one day in the rain.
Then at home in a strife.
He was told by his wife,
'You ought to go out there again!'

There's a woman called Madame Tussaud,
Slow sewers she shows how to sew;
She says, 'If, So-and-so,
You sew so, you'll sew slow,
And you'll only sew so-so, Sew so.'

A distinguished old military Colonel
Once started to publish a jolonel,
But soon it went bust
He gave up in disgust
'For,' said he, 'the expense is infolonel.'

He ordered a porterhouse steak,
Sauerkraut, mince pie and fruit cake
Then sat down to dine,
Drank three kinds of wine,
And retired with a bad stomach ache.

There was a young lad of Calcutta,
Whenever he spoke he would stutter.
To his teacher, said he,
'P-p-lease t-tell me.
Is a b-buttress a f-feminine b-butter?'

A maid who is slightly antique,
Was grossly insulted last wique.
Her best fellow said,
'It is time we were wed,'
And now, it is said, they don't spique.

There was once a maiden named Rhoda,
Who perfectly doted on soda,
She drank so much fizz,
Well, it's none of my biz,
But she's lucky it didn't explode her.

Young Brewster wed Adeline Worcester,
But nobody knew what indorcester
In writing her name
To spell it the same,
And make it read, 'Adeline Brorcester.'

There was a young fellow called Fred
Who seldom had hair on his head
He carried his locks
About in a box
'Because it's the fashion,' he said.

A new servant maid named Mariah,
Had trouble in lighting the fire.
The wood it was green.
So she used gasoline,
Now she sings in the heavenly choir.

A terrible drunkard called Lou
Stole some bottles and drank quite a few
He let out one wild yell.
Then collapsed in a cell,
Thirty days is the time he will do.

There was a fat man they called Falstaff
When he walked he carried a tall staff
And this made him lean —
That is — I mean —
It made him lean on the tall staff.

A fellow who had a toothache,
To a dentist's his way did betake,
But nought could assuage
His grief and his rage.
When the wrong tooth was pulled by mistake.

You've probably heard many times
Of the woman whose parrot did crimes;
Her name was Miss Barrett,
She hadn't a parrot,
But we say that she had 'cause it rhymes.

There was a young lady called Mabel
Who couldn't stand rooms with a gable
If there wasn't another,
She said 'Oh, don't bother,
I'll sleep on the dining room table.'

There was a young man of Belgrade
Who used to catch fish with a spade;
When he'd caught three or four,
He would fling them ashore
Where he fried them in warm lemonade.

There was an old fellow of Lee
Who hid himself under a tree;
When winter came round
He was easily found
For the leaves had come off – don't you see?

There was a young man from Southall
Who went to a fancy dress ball
Information we lack
As to how he got back,
Or whether he got back at all.

There was a young heiress called Rooker,
And a lawyer called Luke, tried to hook her,
But the heiress was shrewd,
Though her question was rude,
Do you look at my looks, Luke, or lucre?

A poet swore several curses,
'For empty,' he said, 'my purse is.
My poems, alack!
Are always sent back.
And my verses are always reverses.'

To write a good modern hymn,
He struggled and scribbled with vymn,
But he put not a bit,
Of pop music in it,
And so its success was but slymn.

A noble young Roman named Caesar
Once called on a maid — tried to squeeze her.
But the girl, with a blush,
Said the Latin for 'Tush,
You horrid young thing! let me be, sir!'

A young lady in crossing the ocean
Grew ill from the ship's dizzy mocean.
She said, with a sigh.
And a tear in her eigh,
'Of living, I've no longer a nocean.'

There was a young lady of Gloucester,
Who married a fellow named Foucester,
But returned to her ma.
And her brother and pa.
Because the man bullied and boucestcr.

There was a young fellow of Lee,
Who went for a swim in the sea;
On a rock (so he said)
He met a mer-maid,
Who offered him afternoon tea.

There was a young lawyer named Leek,
Who sported a prominent beak,
An angry old client
Grew very defiant,
And gave his proboscis a tweak

A lady who warbled in mezzo,
Repined, 'I am always in dezzo,
My runs and my trills
Could pay all my bills
And would, if I didn't forgezzo.'

A fellow who slaughtered two toucans.
Said, 'I shall put them into two cans.'
Two canners who heard,
Said, 'Don't be absurd,
You can't put toucans in two cans.'

There once was a fellow called Mark,
Who called on the comely Miss Clark.
She asked him to stay.
But he answered, 'Nay,
I'm afraid to go home after dark!'

Mr. Bogworthy rented a suite
In a building without any huite.
He lived there for six months,
But never kicked onths.
For a surgeon has cut off his fuite.

A tribesman from rural Australia
Found his society debut a failure
He went to a ball
But was stopped in the hall,
Because of his scanty regalia.

An arab named Abdullah Ben Sharum
Had twenty-four wives in his harem.
When his dearest horse died,
'Mighty Allah!' he cried,
'Take one of my wives - I can spare 'em.'

There once was a cheeky young Mr.,
Who said to a girl when he kr.,
'Won't you please be my wife?'
She said, 'Not on your life;
Please think of me just as your sr.'

A lady who lived in Bel Air
Tried a new-fangled bleach on her hair.
And in just one night.
Her hair got so light,
That her head the next morning was bare.

A cannibal monarch imperial
Kept his wives on a diet of cereal,
But he didn't much care
What the women should wear,
Nor did they; it was quite immaterial.

There was a poor fellow from Lynn,
By accident sat on a pynn,
He let out a shriek,
A howl and a squeak.
And his language was really a synn.

A Turk by the name of Haroun
Ate frozen gin with a spoon.
To one who asked why,
This Turk made reply:
'To drink is forbidden, you loon.'

There was a young lady from Kent,
Who always said just what she meant;
People said, 'She's a dear;
So unique — so sincere' —
But they shunned her by common consent.

Her feelings she could not disguise,
So when he gazed into her uise
So bashfully risen,
He knew she was his'n
And kissed her because he was wuise.

The wise man is strong in his wisdom,
The foolish man weak in his folly;
But the high and the low,
As they come and they go,
Are all easy marks for a jolly.

She's a blonde of the *genus* peroxide
Foolish. If I was here I'd
Let my hair glint
With its natural tint.
Though't were that of a frazzled old foxhide.

A youth with the pride of a czar
Thought it funny to laugh at his cpar,
Till the old man arose
And pummelled his nose.
And showed him full many a cstar.

Said a maid, 'I shall marry for lucre.'
Then her ma stood right up and shuckre,
But just the same
When a chance came
The old dame said no word to rebuchre.

There was a young man from Montana
Who slipped on a peel of banana
He fell on his head
And what he then said,
Was quite the reverse of 'Hosanna'.

An elephant lay in his bunk,
In slumber his chest rose and sunk,
He snored and he snored
Till the jungle folks roared —
Then his wife tied a knot in his trunk.

There was an old sailor of Crete
Whose peg legs propelled him quite neat.
'Strong liquor, he said,
'Never goes to my head,
And I know it can't go to my feet.'

The one silent woman we've known
Sits in Egypt's great desert alone;
And the Egyptian thinks,
As he looks at the Sphynx,
He'd be glad if his wife were of stone.

A beautiful lassie named Florence
Once wept till her tears flowed in torrence.
When asked why she cried,
She sighed and replied,
'The police have been here with some worrence.'

There was a young girl from Westchester
Whose fellow stole up and caressed her.
'Come, kiss me!' he cried.
But she blushed and denied,
And refused to begin till he pressed her.

A chemistry teacher called Luff
While mixing a compounded stuff,
Dropped a match in the vial.
And after a while —
They found his front teeth and one cuff.

There's a lady in Kalamazoo
Who bites all her oysters in two,
For she feels a misgiving,
Should any be living,
They'd kick up a hullabaloo.

There was an old lady named Carr
Who took the 3.3 to Forfar;
For she said: 'I conceive
It is likely to leave
Far before the 4.4 to Forfar.'

There once was a happy hyena
Who played on an old concertina;
He dressed very well,
And in his lapel
He carelessly stuck a verbena.

There once was a baby of yore,
But no one knew what it was for,
And being afraid
It might be mislaid,
They put it away in a drawer.

A young married man of Nunhead,
To a pal very solemnly said:
'Though spliced but a week,
If truth I must speak,
I heartily wish myself dead.'

They played at the game called parchesi
Till he exclaimed: 'This is too easy.
Let's dress and get out
And wander about;'
But the others all thought 'twas too breezy.

There was a young fellow named Phil,
Who courted a charmer named Lil;
Then followed, of course,
A suit for divorce.
So you see he is courting her still.

In Chicago they called her petite,
She'd a figure uncommonly neat;
But of course you can see,
Just as plain as can be.
This didn't apply to her feet.

A man who made photos in platinum
Sat down on some fresh prints to flatinum;
But a pin in the chair
Made him leap up and swear —
Now he wishes he never had satinum.

There once was a schoolboy named Greening,
Who fell down four flights without meaning.
The caretaker swore,
As he struck the ground floor:
'Twill take all the afternoon cleaning.'

A weak but ingenious young guy
Was induced to believe he could fly,
So he built a machine
That required gasoline —
Well, he found it a quick way to die.

Said the mate of this vessel unique
To the cap'n, 'What port shall we seek?'
Said the cap'n, 'We'll dock 'er
In Davy Jones' locker;
The bloomin' old tub's sprung a leak.'

There was a young lady in China,
Who was quite a greedy young diner.
She feasted on snails,
Slugs, peacocks and quails,
'No mixture,' she said, 'could be finer.'

A cheese that was aged and grey
Was walking and talking one day.
Said the cheese, 'Kindly note
My mama was a goat
And I'm made out of curds by the whey.'

There were three little birds in a wood,
Who always sang hymns when they could,
What the words were about
They could never make out.
But they felt they were doing them good.

There was a young man from Darjeeling
Who jumped on a bus bound for Ealing;
It said on the door: 'Don't Spit on the Floor',
So he lay down and spat on the ceiling.

Punctuation's abhorrent to Thomas
And he loathes semicolons and commas
He is such a bad boy
That a wave of great joy
Would arise were the kid taken from us.

A barefoot young woman of Twickenham
Bought shoes 'cause she thought she'd walk quick in 'em;
After walking a mile
She sat on a stile,
And right there became awful sick in 'em.

A teacher whose spelling's unique,
Thus wrote down the days of the week:
The first he spelt 'Sonday,'
The second day 'Munday' —
And now a new teacher they seek.

When the funny man's copy is due,
And jokes seem remarkably few,
He will jump to his chair.
Take a pull at his hair,
Then grind out a limerick or two.

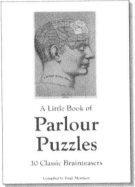
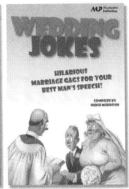

Also available from Montpelier Publishing

Non-Corny Knock Knock Jokes: 150 super funny jokes for kids

More Ripping Riddles and Confounding Conundrums

Riddles in Rhyme

The Bumper Book of Riddles, Puzzles and Rhymes

After Dinner Laughs: jokes and funny stories for speech makers

Wedding Jokes: Hilarious Gags for your Best Man's Speech

Made in the USA
San Bernardino, CA
23 January 2018